MORNING MANTRAS

MORNING MANTRAS

TO INSPIRE YOUR DAY

CICO BOOKS

LONDON NEW YORK

Published in 2016 by CICO Books

An imprint of Ryland Peters & Small Ltd

20–21 Jockey's Fields 341 E 116th St
London WC1R 4BW   New York, NY 10029

www.rylandpeters.com

10 9 8 7 6 5 4 3 2 1

Design © CICO Books 2016

For photography credits,
see pages 142–144.

A CIP catalog record for this book is
available from the Library of Congress
and the British Library.

ISBN: 978-1-78249-340-2

Printed in China

Commissioning editor: Kristine Pidkameny
Senior editor: Carmel Edmonds
Designer: Paul Tilby
Art director: Sally Powell
Production controller: David Hearn
Publishing manager: Penny Craig
Publisher: Cindy Richards

INTRODUCTION

Within this book you will find carefully selected words, mantras, and quotations that will inspire, motivate, and empower you.

Start your day with renewed energy and a fresh outlook. Some mantras will help you to focus on success—what are your goals, and how can you achieve them? Others encourage you to nurture and cherish your relationships, not only with family and friends, but also with yourself. Among these are words that simply remind you to be grateful and to make the most of every moment.

You can use the stylishly presented mantras in a number of ways. You may wish to read one every morning so the thought stays with you throughout the day, or just dip into the book when you feel you need a new perspective. Try pinning up your favorites in your home or workplace for daily inspiration. You could even send them to friends or family when they need a boost.

EMBRACE THE DAY...
YOUR LIFE GETS BETTER WHEN YOU DO.

REACH FOR WHAT
YOU THINK
IS UNREACHABLE

ADVENTURE IS WAITING FOR YOU

IT'S STILL FREE TO DREAM

LOVE NOT WHAT YOU ARE, BUT WHAT YOU MAY BECOME

Miguel de Cervantes

THERE ARE TWO DAYS
IN EVERY THREE OVER
WHICH WE HAVE NO
CONTROL: YESTERDAY
AND TOMORROW.
TODAY IS THE ONLY DAY
THAT WE CAN CHANGE.

TODAY
I
CHOOSE
JOY

DESTINY'S
CALLING

MAKE NEW FRIENDS,
BUT KEEP THE OLD:
ONE IS SILVER,
THE OTHER IS GOLD

THE ONLY WAY TO HAVE A FRIEND
IS TO BE ONE

Ralph Waldo Emerson

THE MOST RELIABLE
WAY TO PREDICT
THE FUTURE IS
TO CREATE IT

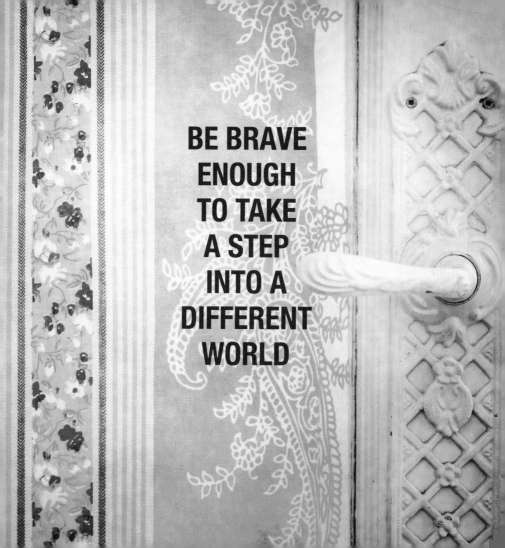

BE BRAVE
ENOUGH
TO TAKE
A STEP
INTO A
DIFFERENT
WORLD

LIFE IS LIKE THE OCEAN—
IT'S ALWAYS BEAUTIFUL

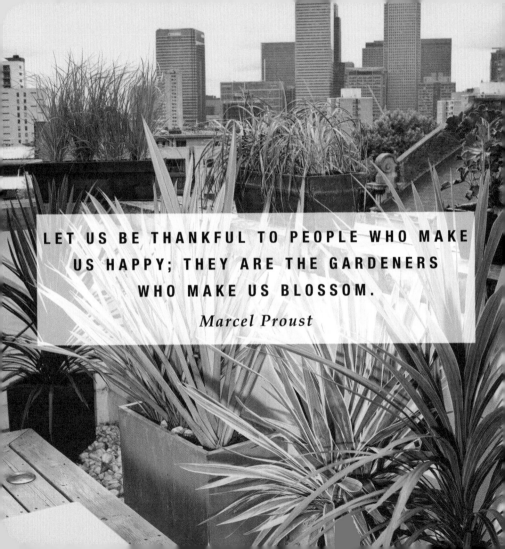

LET US BE THANKFUL TO PEOPLE WHO MAKE
US HAPPY; THEY ARE THE GARDENERS
WHO MAKE US BLOSSOM.

Marcel Proust

**WHEREVER YOU GO,
GO WITH
ALL YOUR HEART**

Confucius

We must have perseverance and above all confidence in ourselves. We must believe that we are gifted for something, and that this thing, at whatever cost, must be attained.

Marie Curie

LIFE
IS
TOUGH
BUT
SO
ARE
YOU

I've realized that every time I thought

I was being rejected from something

good, I was actually being

redirected to something better

Imam al-Ghazali

DO ALL THE GOOD YOU CAN, BY ALL THE MEANS YOU CAN, IN ALL THE WAYS YOU CAN, IN ALL THE PLACES YOU CAN, AT ALL THE TIMES YOU CAN, TO ALL THE PEOPLE YOU CAN, AS LONG AS EVER YOU CAN

HOWEVER LONG THE NIGHT, THE DAY WILL BREAK

WORKING TOGETHER IS ALWAYS EASIER THAN WORKING ALONE

OPEN YOUR EYES AND SEE
THE BEAUTY THAT SURROUNDS YOU

THERE IS NOTHING MORE PRECIOUS THAN TIME

Saint Bernardino of Siena

AMAZE
YOURSELF
TODAY

BE FEARLESS

IN THE

PURSUIT OF

WHAT SETS

YOUR SOUL

ON FIRE

TO BEGIN,
BEGIN

STORMS DON'T LAST FOREVER

STOP THINKING AND JUST LET THINGS HAPPEN

WHAT'S
MEANT
FOR YOU
WON'T
PASS
YOU BY

BE

HAPPY

FOR

THIS

MOMENT

Omar
Khayyam

FOCUS ON WHAT MATTERS TODAY

LOVE ALL, TRUST A FEW, DO WRONG TO NONE

William Shakespeare

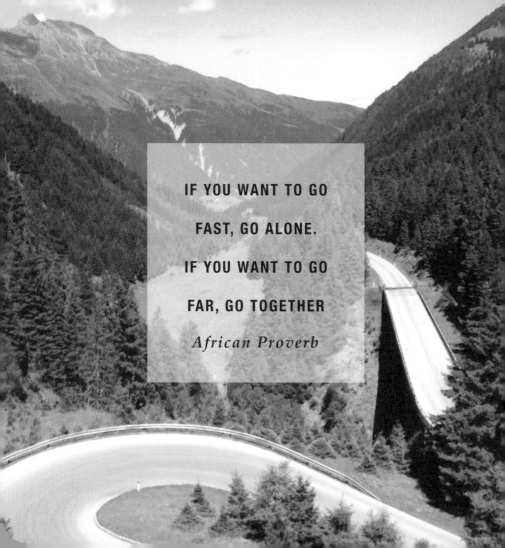

IF YOU WANT TO GO

FAST, GO ALONE.

IF YOU WANT TO GO

FAR, GO TOGETHER

African Proverb

MAKE IT HAPPEN

LIVE
ALL YOU CAN
IT'S A MISTAKE
NOT TO

Henry James

TRUST YOUR INSTINCT

DO SOMETHING
EVERY DAY
THAT BRINGS
YOU CLOSER
TO YOUR GOALS

NEVER PUT
THE KEY
TO YOUR
HAPPINESS
IN SOMEONE
ELSE'S POCKET

GIVE MORE THAN YOU RECEIVE

INTENTION
MANIFESTS
CHANGE

INVIGORATE YOUR DAY

THE ONLY PERSON YOU SHOULD TRY TO BE BETTER THAN IS THE PERSON YOU WERE YESTERDAY

HAVE BIG DREAMS:
YOU WILL GROW INTO THEM

NO BEAUTY
SHINES
BRIGHTER
THAN THAT
OF A
GOOD HEART

FEED YOUR FOCUS

DO EVERYTHING

WITH LOVE

1 Corinthians 16:14

A GRATEFUL HEART IS A
MAGNET FOR MIRACLES

LOVE YOURSELF

GOOD PEOPLE BRING OUT THE GOOD IN PEOPLE

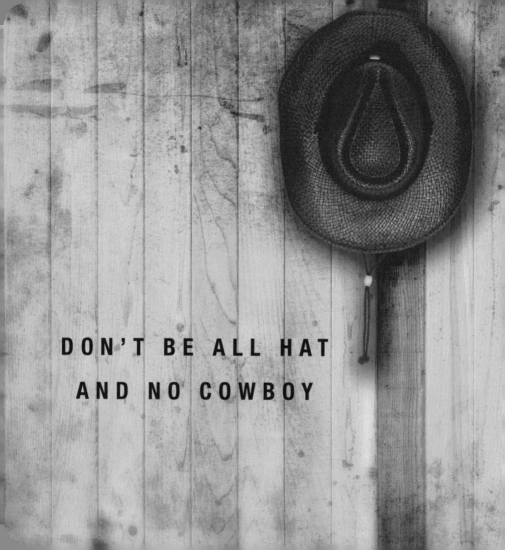

BE THE TYPE OF
PERSON
THAT YOU WANT
TO MEET

ONE
DAY
AT
A
TIME

ALL GLORY COMES FROM DARING TO BEGIN

Eugene F. Ware

LIFE IS A ONE-TIME OFFER —USE IT WELL

JUST BECAUSE IT ISN'T HAPPENING NOW DOESN'T MEAN IT NEVER WILL

**DON'T CALL IT A DREAM.
CALL IT A PLAN**

SOME THINGS MAY CATCH YOUR EYE,
BUT PURSUE ONLY THOSE
THAT CAPTURE YOUR HEART

Ancient Indian Proverb

NEVER LET A STUMBLE IN THE ROAD
BE THE END OF THE JOURNEY

APPRECIATE WHAT YOU HAVE

YOUR LIFE ONLY
GETS BETTER
WHEN YOU DO

BE CALM TODAY

**ATTRACT WHAT
YOU WANT
BY BEING
WHAT YOU WANT**

WE HAVE TWO EARS AND ONE
MOUTH SO THAT WE CAN LISTEN
TWICE AS MUCH AS WE SPEAK

Epictetus

MAKE SPACE FOR YOUR DREAMS

IT IS NOT HAPPY PEOPLE WHO ARE THANKFUL. IT IS THANKFUL PEOPLE WHO ARE HAPPY

YOU DESERVE GOOD THINGS

DON'T WAIT FOR THE PERFECT MOMENT—TAKE THE MOMENT AND MAKE IT PERFECT

TRUST THAT WHEN THE ANSWER IS NO, THERE'S A BETTER YES DOWN THE ROAD

WAKE UP. KICK ASS. BE KIND. REPEAT

BROKEN CRAYONS STILL COLOR

WORRY NOT
THAT
NO ONE
KNOWS YOU;
SEEK TO
BE WORTH
KNOWING

Confucius

HAPPINESS IS FOUND WHEN YOU STOP COMPARING YOURSELF TO OTHER PEOPLE

REMEMBER TO LISTEN

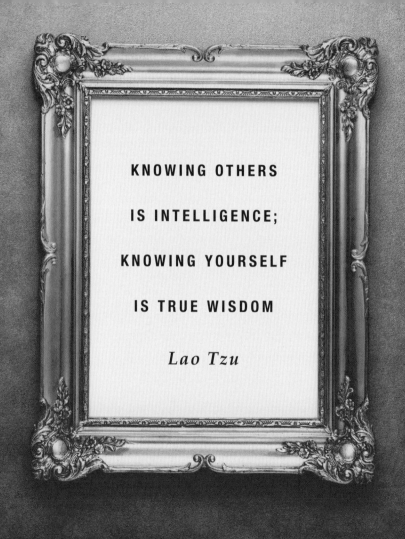

KNOWING OTHERS

IS INTELLIGENCE;

KNOWING YOURSELF

IS TRUE WISDOM

Lao Tzu

I'M NOT BEAUTIFUL
LIKE YOU;
I'M BEAUTIFUL
LIKE ME.

KEEP YOUR EYES ON THE STARS

AND YOUR FEET ON THE GROUND

Theodore Roosevelt

STUMBLING BLOCKS ARE SIMPLY STEPPING STONES IN DISGUISE

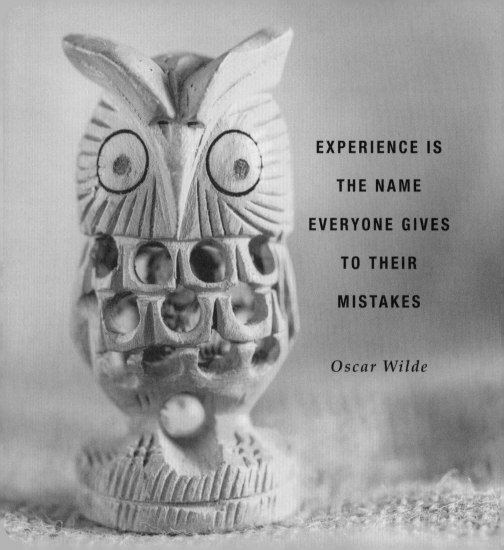

EXPERIENCE IS
THE NAME
EVERYONE GIVES
TO THEIR
MISTAKES

Oscar Wilde

A SMOOTH SEA NEVER MADE A SKILLED SAILOR

WE KNOW WHAT WE ARE NOW, BUT
NOT WHAT WE MAY BECOME

William Shakespeare

**PERFECT PEOPLE AREN'T REAL.
REAL PEOPLE AREN'T PERFECT**

BE THE KIND OF
LEADER
THAT YOU WOULD
FOLLOW

BE THE SUN TODAY AND SEE WHAT YOU ATTRACT

NOTE TO SELF: I'M GOING TO MAKE YOU SO PROUD

MAKE TODAY SO AWESOME

THAT YESTERDAY GETS JEALOUS

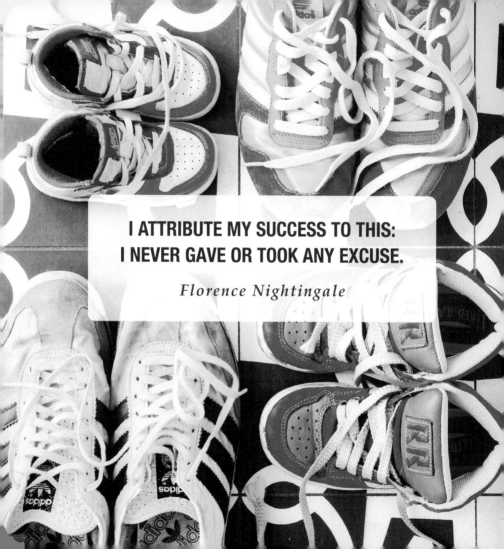

I ATTRIBUTE MY SUCCESS TO THIS:
I NEVER GAVE OR TOOK ANY EXCUSE.

Florence Nightingale

LET GO OF YOUR PAST IF YOU WANT
TO CHANGE YOUR FUTURE

BE WHO YOU WANT TO BE, NOT WHAT OTHERS WANT TO SEE

A BEAUTIFUL LIFE BEGINS WITH A BEAUTIFUL MIND

LIFE HAS TWO RULES:

NUMBER 1
NEVER QUIT

NUMBER 2
ALWAYS REMEMBER
RULE NUMBER 1

CONQUER ANGER WITH NON-ANGER. CONQUER BADNESS WITH GOODNESS. CONQUER MEANNESS WITH GENEROSITY. CONQUER DISHONESTY WITH TRUTH

The Buddha

WHAT YOU ALLOW IS WHAT WILL CONTINUE

FALL SEVEN TIMES, STAND UP EIGHT

Japanese Proverb

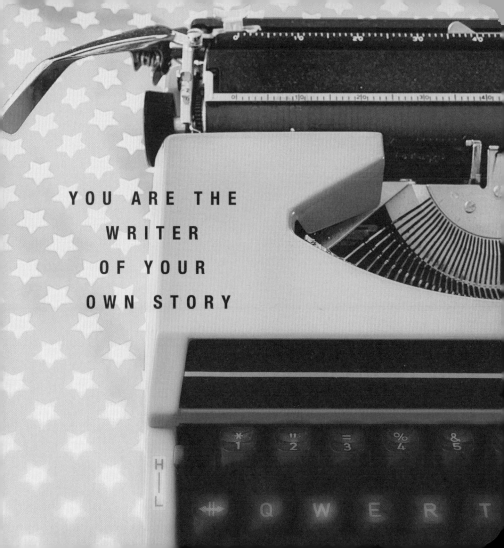

YOU ARE THE
WRITER
OF YOUR
OWN STORY

LIGHT
TOMORROW
WITH
TODAY

Elizabeth Barrett Browning

EVERYTHING YOU'VE EVER WANTED IS ON THE OTHER SIDE OF FEAR

George Adair

YOU CAN'T START THE
NEXT CHAPTER OF YOUR
LIFE IF YOU KEEP
RE-READING THE
LAST ONE

YOUR VIBE
ATTRACTS
YOUR TRIBE

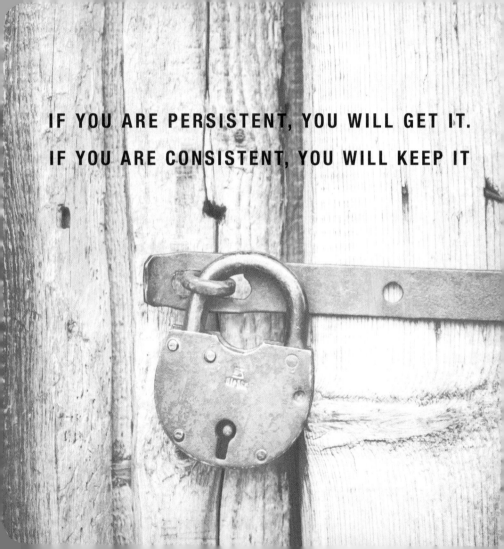

IF YOU ARE PERSISTENT, YOU WILL GET IT.
IF YOU ARE CONSISTENT, YOU WILL KEEP IT

BE YOUR OWN HERO

IT IS NEVER

TOO LATE

TO BE THE

PERSON

YOU MIGHT

HAVE BEEN

ALWAYS WEAR YOUR
INVISIBLE CROWN

FOCUS
ON
THE
GOOD

FOR EVERY MINUTE YOU ARE ANGRY, YOU LOSE 60 SECONDS OF HAPPINESS

Ralph Waldo Emerson

BE KIND TO YOURSELF

KNOW YOUR WORTH

OLD WAYS
WON'T OPEN
NEW DOORS

WAKE UP
AND BE
PURPOSEFUL

DREAM BIG

IF YOU AVOID CONFLICT TO KEEP THE PEACE,

YOU START A WAR WITHIN YOURSELF

SOME DAYS YOU HAVE TO CREATE YOUR OWN SUNSHINE

BE STRONGER
THAN YOUR EXCUSES

I CAN AND I WILL

DO NOT COMPARE YOURSELF TO OTHERS

CHOOSE TO BE UNSTOPPABLE

THE ONLY
PERSON
RESPONSIBLE
FOR YOUR
HAPPINESS
IS YOU

EMBRACE THE DAY

DO EVERYTHING

TODAY

WITH INTENTION

EVERYTHING WILL BE FINE IN THE END IF IT'S NOT FINE, IT'S NOT THE END

SET YOUR GOAL, MAKE A PLAN, AND STICK TO IT

IF YOU FEEL LIKE YOU
DESERVE BETTER,
IT'S BECAUSE YOU DO

DO THINGS THAT MAKE YOU FEEL EXCITED

SOURCES AND ACKNOWLEDGMENTS

Every effort has been made to acknowledge sources,
but the publishers would be glad to hear of any omissions.

Page 15 "The only way to have a friend is to be one."
Ralph Waldo Emerson, *Essays* (1841), "Of Friendship"

Page 22 "We must have perseverance and above all confidence in ourselves. We must believe that we are gifted for something, and that this thing, at whatever cost, must be attained."
Marie Curie, as quoted in *Madame Curie: A Biography* (1937) by Eve Curie Labouisse

Page 39 "Love all, trust a few, do wrong to none."
William Shakespeare, *All's Well That Ends Well* (1604–1605)

Page 42 "Live all you can; it's a mistake not to."
Henry James, *The Ambassadors* (1903), book V, ch. II.

Page 74 "We have two ears and one mouth so that we can listen twice as much as we speak."
Epictetus, *The Golden Sayings of Epictetus*, trans. by Hastings Crossley. Vol. II, Part 2. The Harvard Classics. New York: P.F. Collier & Son (1909–14); Bartleby.com (2001)

Page 86 "Knowing others is intelligence; knowing yourself is true wisdom."
Lao Tzu, *Tao Te Ching*

Page 90 "Experience is the name everyone gives to their mistakes."
Oscar Wilde, *Vera; or, The Nihilists* (1880)

Page 105 "Conquer anger with non-anger. Conquer badness with goodness. Conquer meanness with generosity. Conquer dishonesty with truth."
The Buddha, *The Dhammapada*

Page 110 "Light tomorrow with today."
Elizabeth Barrett Browning, "The Romance of the Swan's Nest" in *Women Poets of the Nineteenth Century* (1907, ed. Alfred H. Miles)

PICTURE CREDITS

KEY: *ph* = photographer

Front cover © Ryland Peters and Small/ *ph* Addie Chinn

Back cover © Simon Wint (simonwint.com)

Page 1 © CICO Books/*ph* Gavin Kingcome

Page 2 © Kirsty Seymour-Ure: follow her on Instagram @kirstyinitaly

Page 3 Shutterstock/© tomertu

Page 4 Shutterstock/© Stokkete

Page 6 Shutterstock/© William Perugini

Page 7 © Kirsty Seymour-Ure: follow her on Instagram @kirstyinitaly

Page 8 © Kirsty Seymour-Ure: follow her on Instagram @kirstyinitaly

Page 11 © Alessio Grain: follow him on Instagram @grain_ap

Page 12 © CICO Books/*ph* Simon Brown

Page 13 © Kirsty Seymour-Ure: follow her on Instagram @kirstyinitaly

Page 14 © Ryland Peters and Small/ *ph* Debi Treloar

Page 17 © CICO Books/*ph* Caroline Arber

Page 18 © Ryland Peters and Small/ *ph* Debi Treloar

Page 19 © CICO Books/*ph* Caroline Arber

Page 20 © CICO Books/*ph* Amanda Darcy

Page 21 © Ryland Peters and Small/ *ph* Ian Wallace

Page 23 © Simon Wint (simonwint.com)

Page 24 © Simon Wint (simonwint.com)

Page 27 © Simon Wint (simonwint.com)

Page 29 Shutterstock/© Carsten Reisinger

Page 30 © CICO Books/*ph* Mark Scott

Page 33 © Ryland Peters and Small/ *ph* Catherine Gratwicke

Page 34 Shutterstock/© Lucas Nishimoto

Page 35 © CICO Books/*ph* Penny Wincer

Page 36 © Simon Wint (simonwint.com)

Page 37 Shutterstock/© xtock

Page 39 © Kirsty Seymour-Ure: follow her on Instagram @kirstyinitaly

Page 40 © Simon Wint (simonwint.com)

Page 41 © Simon Wint (simonwint.com)

Page 43 © Ryland Peters and Small/ *ph* Paul Massey

Page 45 © CICO Books/*ph* Penny Wincer

Page 46 Shutterstock/© Anna-Mari West

Page 47 Shutterstock/© Zemler

Page 49 © CICO Books/*ph* Gavin Kingcome

Page 51 Shutterstock/© qoppi

Page 52 © CICO Books/*ph* Amanda Darcy

Page 53 © Ryland Peters and Small/ *ph* Lena Ikse Bergman

Page 54 © Ryland Peters and Small/ *ph* Debi Treloar

Page 55 © Ryland Peters and Small/ *ph* William Reavell

Page 56 © CICO Books/*ph* Christopher Drake

Page 57 © CICO Books/*ph* Emma Mitchell

Page 58 © Ryland Peters and Small/ *ph* Christopher Drake

Page 60 Shutterstock/© Hannamariah

Page 61 © Ryland Peters and Small/ *ph* Polly Wreford

Page 63 Shutterstock/© Elya Vatel

Page 66 © CICO Books/*ph* David Merewether

Page 67 © Ryland Peters and Small/ *ph* Jan Baldwin

Page 68 © Ryland Peters and Small/ *ph* Chris Tubbs

Page 69 © Kirsty Seymour-Ure: follow her on Instagram @kirstyinitaly

Page 71 Shutterstock/© Om Yos

Page 72 © Kirsty Seymour-Ure: follow her on Instagram @kirstyinitaly